THE EIGHT PRINCIPLES OF FAITH

THE EIGHT PRINCIPLES OF FAITH

LENONA L. LAUREANO

XULON PRESS ELITE

Xulon Press
2301 Lucien Way #415
Maitland, FL 32751
407.339.4217
www.xulonpress.com

© 2021 by Lenona L. Laureano

All rights reserved solely by the author. The author guarantees all contents are original and do not infringe upon the legal rights of any other person or work. No part of this book may be reproduced in any form without the permission of the author. The views expressed in this book are not necessarily those of the publisher.

Due to the changing nature of the Internet, if there are any web addresses, links, or URLs included in this manuscript, these may have been altered and may no longer be accessible. The views and opinions shared in this book belong solely to the author and do not necessarily reflect those of the publisher. The publisher therefore disclaims responsibility for the views or opinions expressed within the work.

Unless otherwise indicated, Scripture quotations taken from the King James Version (KJV) – *public domain.*

Scripture quotations taken from the Holy Bible, New Living Translation (NLT). Copyright ©1996, 2004, 2007 by Tyndale House Foundation. Used by permission of Tyndale House Publishers, Inc.

Printed in the United States of America

Paperback ISBN-13: 978-1-6628-1543-0
Ebook ISBN-13: 978-1-6628-1544-7

PRINCIPLE

A guiding sense of requirements, rules, and obligations that will lead to the right conduct and actions.

DEDICATION

This booklet is dedicated to every born-again believer.

Jeremiah 29:11

INTRODUCTION

The Lord spoke to me in a dream and said, *"Write a booklet on the Eight Principles of Faith."* In obedience to what He said, this booklet was produced.

In all honesty, I didn't understand what He was talking about. I would think of faith comes by hearing and hearing by the word of God (Romans 10:17), thinking that *hearing* could be a principle.

I thought about faith works by love (Galatians 5:6), thinking that *love* could be a principle. As I continued to search the scriptures, the Holy Spirit led me to 2 Peter. In fact, *love* ended up being a principle.

I asked the Lord, right before the publishing of this booklet, *"Why do you want me to write this."* It wasn't a long drawn-out statement, He just gave me a scripture.

> **Being born-again, not of corruptible seed, but of incorruptible, by the word of God, which liveth and abideth forever. (1 Peter 1:23 KJV).**

You see, Peter was writing to believers who were under a great deal of persecution, removed from their homes, and scattered throughout five regions of the earth.

They needed understanding and encouragement regarding the situations they were in. As in any devastation, you need to be reminded of who you are and mindful of your purpose. You are born-again. You have accepted Jesus Christ as your Savior. You are now born from an incorruptible seed, which is the word of God.

Born-again believers go through trying times, but we need to remember that God has a plan for us (Jeremiah 29:11). No matter what you are going through, God's plan is always good. We may not like it, but it's good.

1 Peter 4:13 clearly says that we will be partakers in Christ's suffering but know that God will not allow you to go through anything that He did not equip you to handle (1 Corinthians 10:13).

We can do all things through Christ who strengthens us, but we have to go through Christ (Philippians 4:13).

Don't allow anything that is happening on Earth to take you away from the love that God has for you. For God so loved the

Introduction

world that He gave His only Son and all who believe in His Son will have everlasting life (John 3:16).

As ambassadors of Christ, we have a responsibility on this Earth to save souls. Let's not get caught up in our situations, as this is a trick of the enemy. I'm not saying don't take care of what's going on in your life. I'm saying cast all your cares upon the Lord because He cares for you (1 Peter 5:7).

I'm saying take no thought for your life (Matthew 6:25-34). Let's seek the Lord while He may be found. Let's call upon Him while He's near (Isaiah 55:6).

These Christians were suffering. Peter was reminding them that they are only strangers and pilgrims on the earth, and the suffering they are experiencing is nothing compared to the glory that will be revealed when Jesus returns (1 Peter 1:1-4).

The Bible was written for our learning, and we have to apply the scriptures to get through life. We are here on Earth just passing through. At whatever age you will be when God calls you home is just a drop in the bucket compared to eternity that awaits us.

We have to be mindful that being born-again is not a garment that we can take off. We are born-again at work, we are born-again at the grocery store, and we are born-again sitting in traffic. Wherever we go, wherever we are, we are born-again.

I pray that your life will be blessed even more as you continue to read through this reminder of God's word.

CHAPTER ONE
DILIGENCE

The first principle we will be discussing is diligence. This word is very powerful and carries a lot of weight. My definition of diligence is being persistent, tenacious, going hard and strong in what area you decide to place it in.

In this particular case, Peter was encouraging the believers to be diligent in supplementing, adding to, and enhancing their faith with virtue, knowledge, temperance, patience, godliness, brotherly kindness, and love during the situation they were in.

Peter was diligently reinforcing scriptures in the heart of these born-again believers. They were going through a storm. The key to getting through any storm is to keep your mind stayed on God. God says if you keep your mind stayed on me, you _will_ have perfect peace (Isaiah 26:3).

If you look at storms, doubt will kick in and you will begin to sink (Matthew 14:28-31).

I know this is easy to understand and so hard to do, but God has truly given us all things to succeed in life while possessing a life of godliness. This means that we will conquer any situation that comes our way.

We are more than conquerors. We are the light of the world. We may be the only hope for the lost. If the world sees us struggling with God, what hope is there for them?

We are born-again of an incorruptible seed. We have to live as such. Who can defeat God? Who can stand against Him? Name one situation that God did not overcome.

If you feel like you are being defeated. Stop. Repent. Get in the word and out of your head.

We have to be diligent in building up our faith (Jude 1:20).

The Bible was written for our learning (Romans 15:4). It is our blueprint for succeeding in this life. We cannot make it without it. The word of God is a lamp unto our feet and a light that keeps us on the right path (Psalm 119:105).

If a person stops going hard for Christ, there is a door that will open for the enemy to come in. The devil is so subtle, and we have to make sure that we do not give him any room to deceive us.

One thing about diligence is that it never stops. It's aggressive and persistent. Did you come across that point in your walk with God when you lost your persistency in following Him?

If you look back at that time, I guarantee you that it had something to do with your feelings. Did you know that your feelings will get you into a whole lot of trouble?

You cannot be an effective Christian by consistently, tenaciously (diligently) walking in your emotions. You will live an up-and-down life. Paul said that he keeps under his body and brings it into subjection (1 Corinthians 9:27).

For a person to keep under their body, will require them to have a heart of diligence. We can't faint every time things do not go the way we want. Sad to say, but it's never going to be the way we want because <u>Jesus</u> is the *way*, the *truth*, and the *life* (John 14:6).

Let me explain something. You have to change the program in your mind. If you were a coach, you cannot go into the game with the same plays because the opposing coach will catch on to your strategy and win the game every time.

As born-again believers, we cannot go into Christianity with worldly plays, because we will be defeated every time. God's ways are not our ways and neither are His thoughts our thoughts (Isaiah 55:8).

And for the one who is diligently trying to make God change and convert to the way you want Him to be, it's not going to happen. He's God and He changes not (Malachi 3:6).

God has made it very clear to us that He is the same, yesterday, today, and will be the same forever (Hebrews 13:8).

Keep your heart with all diligence no matter what and watch what God will do for you.

REFLECT ON THIS

Are you willing to suffer for being a Christian?

Will you continue to be faithful to God, even if things do not go your way?

Are you ready to supplement your faith with virtue, knowledge, temperance, patience, godliness, brotherly kindness, and love?

CHAPTER TWO
VIRTUE

God wants us to watch how we present our personalities around others. If we are born-again believers, we have to carry ourselves a certain way, not that we are better than anyone, which certainly is not the case.

Virtue is possessing a spirit of excellence. How we walk, talk and carry ourselves, should be with a spirit of excellence. We have to be upright and sincere. We have to stand and support what is upright, sincere, honest, and true. God is letting us know that the same character of excellence He has is the same spirit of excellence we should have.

Job was a man of integrity. Even amid his suffering, he kept himself. He didn't say what he felt. Why? Because he had a working knowledge of God. You see, the only way you are going to be able to act a certain way, talk a certain way, live a certain way is to be able to allow the word of God to become effective in your life.

It's like this, you accept Jesus Christ into your heart and instantly your spirit becomes alive unto God, thereby making you born-again. You still have the same heart, mind, soul, feelings, emotions, and attitude but there is something different about you.

When your spirit becomes alive, God automatically removes things from your life. Some things you may notice right away, other things you will notice as you go on. From that point, you have to become familiar with the Bible. The Bible is your blueprint for building a virtuous life in Christ. You will never be able to live a life that is pleasing to God by what's in your mind, feelings, and beliefs. People are very opinionated when it comes down to spiritual things.

People have their own beliefs, just like we've had our own beliefs before we found out the truth. If you don't read your Bible, the influence of some else's belief will mix in with your personal beliefs and cloud the truth.

This is why the Bible says you will know the truth and the truth will make you free (John 8:32). You will only know the truth when you get rid of your personal beliefs and study the scriptures.

People have their own opinions about the Bible, saying that man wrote it. Yes, man did write the Bible, but not only that, man published, produced, and sold millions of copies of it and millions of versions of it too.

One thing is missing from that statement, and make sure you educated them saying:

> "**All scripture is given by inspiration of God** and is profitable for doctrine, for reproof, for correction, for instructions in righteousness. **2 Peter 3:16, KJV**"

The devil has trained people to leave this part out. You know why? Because the Bible exposes sin, just like the name of Jesus exposes sin. If the devil convinces someone to downplay the Bible by saying it's written by man, then their sin will not be exposed, thereby causing them to die in their sin. That's satan's number one goal.

Men and women were inspired by the Spirit of God to write, not their words, but words that were given to them by God. How is this possible? You just have to get to know Him. This can all happen as you set aside some time of devotion to read, pray and talk with God.

You just can't read your bible, walk away and act as though you haven't read it. Let's take a look at James 1:22, 25 KJV:

> "*But be ye doers of the word, and not hearers only, deceiving your own selves. But whoso looketh into the perfect law of liberty and continueth therein, he being not a forgetful hearer, but a doer of the work, this man shall be blessed in his deed.*"

We have to do the Bible. This is the only way we are going to be able to understand God and live a virtuous life. James stated that you have to do the word of God. You have to look at it intently and do it. You can't make excuses for not doing the Bible. Your feelings are not going to just let you live out scriptures, you have to make yourself live the Bible way.

Virtue, excellence, will only be active in our lives the more we give ourselves to the word of God and allow the word of God to change us. If the Bible was not necessary, we will not have it today.

Are you going to feel like reading the Bible? No.

Are you going to continue to let your feelings and emotions keep you from reading the Bible? Unfortunately, that choice is ours.

Let's do our very best to represent Christ to the world and be excellent in everything that we do.

REFLECT ON THIS

Are you willing to live a life of virtue?

Will you lay your beliefs down and pick up God's word?

How do you see yourself presented to the world?

CHAPTER THREE
KNOWLEDGE

We have to enhance our faith with Biblical knowledge. I have said earlier that we all have our own opinions and beliefs about things. We feel that what we believe is right, but this is wrong. As born-again believers, we don't have the privilege of keeping our own beliefs.

> ***"Therefore if any man be in Christ, he is a new creature; old things are passed away, behold all things are become new, and all things are of God who hath reconciled us to himself by Jesus Christ and hath given us the ministry of reconciliation. 2 Corinthians 5:17-18, KJV)".***

You see: "old things are passed away." This includes our old ways, habits, and beliefs. Before Christ, we relied on this way of living, and now *with* Christ, we have to rely on the new way of living—the Bible way of living.

We can't go on living and having a concept of what Christianity is. We can't continue believing that we know all about God.

The only way we will know who God is, is by developing a relationship with Him, just like we have developed relationships with our best friends, coworkers, neighbors, and spouses.

When you first met your best friend, you just didn't look at them and say, "Yeah, I know all about them, their favorite color, favorite food, and favorite team." No. You gained all of that information when you spent time getting to know them.

The only way, we are going to have a working knowledge of God is by sitting down and getting to know Him through the Bible. It will be strange at first, but you will get used to it with a little patience.

Have you ever heard someone say, "I'm being transparent with you"? In other words, they are trying to let you know that nothing is being withheld from you and that they are being as truthful as they can be.

God has been transparent with us from the very beginning since He inspired men to write about Him. He didn't leave anything out.

We can say, "I'm being transparent" and withhold some things we don't want to be exposed.

God did not do that. He has allowed us to see what He likes and doesn't like. What He wants us to do or not do. What He wants us to touch or not touch.

Knowledge

He even tells us how we are to approach Him. He said, come boldly to the throne of grace (Hebrews 4:16).

He loves us so much, but we allow our feelings to interpret God's love for us. We would rather believe our feelings, which can change at the drop of a hat, rather than believe God, who was here from the very beginning. Just in case it slipped your mind, He did create Heaven and Earth.

Did you also know that God will bring you into the wilderness so you can get to know Him? If He did it to Jesus, don't you think He will do it to us? Being in the wilderness will cause you to see somethings about yourself. This is what was going on with these born-again believers.

I thought I had a working knowledge of God until I had to enter into the wilderness. Let me tell you, I had to learn about Him real quick in order for me to survive that experience.

Jesus was led into the wilderness to be tempted by the devil (Matthew 4:1). Sometimes we are led into our wilderness to grow. The more you get to know God, the more <u>you will need</u> to grow, read Luke 12:48.

Your wilderness could consist of some sort of pain and suffering. The knowledge I possessed was nothing compared to the knowledge I've learned when the Lord brought me out. I knew that the only way I was going to make it, was to lean on the word of God.

God has manifested Himself to me so much so that I have a working knowledge of Him and His word to be a conqueror in any area of my life. Did not He say that you are more than conquers (Romans 8:37)? You need the word of God in you to believe that.

God will give you weapons to be successful in your battles with the devil. The devil comes to steal, kill and destroy but Jesus comes to give us life and that more abundantly (John 10:10).

Get to know God. Be diligent and determined to understand who He is and stop allowing the enemy to detour us into something that is meaningless.

REFLECT ON THIS

If God led you into an uncomfortable situation, would you run to the Bible and endure it?

Are you ready to search the scriptures and learn about God?

Will you continue to rely on your beliefs?

CHAPTER FOUR
TEMPERANCE

Temperance is displaying an act of self-control and it's also one of the fruits of the Holy Spirit. The Holy Spirit can enable you to have this fruit of temperance (self-control) in full operation in your life.

God is the only one who sees you. God looks beyond your physical and sees directly into the heart. He is the only one who knows why you are the way you are. He's the only one who knows how to get you to control yourself.

Most of the time, we lash out because there is something serious going on within us, and we don't know how to express it or become free of it.

The word of God is designed for that. The word of God is designed to go within you and remove that which does not belong. This is why prayer is so vital. Our prayers are already answered even before we get them out of our mouths. (Isaiah 65:24).

Let me interject one thing. Don't pray problems. God already knows about your problems. Find that scripture in the Bible that pertains to your situation.

For example, if you have a problem with fear, get your Bible and pray:

> **God your word says that you have not given me a spirit of fear but you gave me power, love, and a sound mind (2 Timothy 1:7). Spirit of fear, I bind you up in the name of Jesus. I command you to lose your assignment over my life in Jesus' name.**

Don't allow any attribute from the devil to affect your life. If it comes from God, keep it. If it comes from the devil, reject it.

Peter says, "Add temperance, self-control to your faith." You have to make sure that your fuse is lengthened. People who "go off" are considered to be people who have short fuses.

The Bible has about four scriptures on temperance. What more can you add in telling a person to control their attitude.

There are several people in the Bible whom I'm sure had this fruit in operation in their lives. One of them is Job. In all that happened to him, he worshipped God. Job had a good reason to spaz out. He lost his business, he lost his staff and also his children.

Job did not spin out of control yelling, screaming, and cursing God. Job had a working knowledge of God and the spirit of self-control was evident in his life. Why do you say this? Because his wife couldn't understand that after everything that happened Job worshipped God. Self-control was not present when his wife said to curse God and die. Job, with self-control, said, *"shall we receive good from the hand of God and not bad"* (Job 2:9-10).

Self-control was a part of Job's life. If you know who God is, you will come to realize that God will allow you to go through some uncomfortable situations. The secret to that is remembering that He loves you. He will not place you in a situation where He might lose you. He will not allow you to be overtaken in anything, He will always make a way for you to escape (1 Corinthians 10:13).

Another person who maintained a spirit of self-control is Jesus. Jesus could have called a legion of angels to come and protect Him from the abuse of men, but it was love that went to the cross for mankind. It was temperance and self-control, which was active in Jesus' life to be able to endure that suffering for us.

If Jesus did not complete that mission, mankind would have been separated from God forever.

Adam and Eve were kicked out of the Garden of Eden not because God was being mean. God was protecting them from touching the tree of life in a sinful state because they would have lived a life separated from God forever (Genesis 3:22-24).

It may sound like a bad thing for God to remove things or people away from your life, but as you get to know Him, you will understand His reasons for allowing things.

REFLECT ON THIS

Would you possess a spirit of self-control if God allowed you to lose your only source of income?

If God called your loved-one home, would you walk away from Him?

Do you have a problem "lashing out" in situations that come your way?

CHAPTER FIVE
PATIENCE

The first scripture that comes to mind is:

"But let patience have her perfect work, that you may be perfect and entire wanting nothing, James 1:4 KJV."

Patience has work to do within us, and we will never know the outcome if we don't let patience complete its job.

You see, the Bible will be a foreign thing to you if you don't allow its words to be effective in your life.

Patience is needed during trying times. People don't like to go through hardship and pain. It's during those moments that if you be patient, step out on faith, and take God at His word, it will all make sense.

I mentioned earlier that God will not allow the devil to overtake you. You just have to know that He is God and He's got you.

Some people have support teams, such as a friend, parent, or a professional, but in all of their advice, they cannot see or reach deep enough to bring peace to your life.

We don't like to wait. The preparation of fast foods has conditioned us not to wait. I'm sure the intent was to have the ability to produce good quality food in a short amount of time, but we took it too far.

People are so conditioned to having the ability to order food through the speaker, drive around to the window, grab their food, and head to their destination.

It doesn't work like that in the body of Christ. Don't get me wrong, God can do quick work, but we have to experience the process so we will understand. How are we going to help anyone if we never go through anything?

The work is done but the manifestation takes a little time and this is where people grow faint and backslide because it's taking too long.

Patience *will bring* you to a place of maturity. Patience will become that peace in your life causing you to want for nothing.

I remember when I wanted a husband. I wanted a husband so bad that this would be the only thing I would think about.

Patience

I would talk to God about having a husband so much hoping that my explanation of why I needed one, will convince Him to give me one right away.

I got so frustrated waiting on God that I just gave up. I knew what God wanted from me at the time, but I wasn't ready to give it to Him. God was waiting on me to give myself totally and completely over to Him.

Most of the time, if not all of the time, God wants us. That husband wasn't coming just yet because it was time for me to strengthen my relationship with God.

We have to come to realize that just as much as we <u>want</u> from God, God wants just as much from us.

I began to go after God as if He was getting away. I got so serious with Him at this point that my desire for a husband was completely gone. The love that I wanted from man was hidden in God.

He just wanted me. Like He just wants you.

We should give all desires to God and say if I get blessed with it or not, I still want God to manage my life. I will love Him with or without obtaining my desires.

If we don't allow patience to work within us, we will lose out on a relationship with God. We just have to get to a place in our lives and figure out what's more important, pleasing God or pleasing self.

REFLECT ON THIS

Have you given yourself totally over to God?

Do you have a time limit on things you are waiting for?

Is patience being reflected in your life?

CHAPTER SIX
GODLINESS

God has given us all things that pertain to life and Godliness (2 Peter 1:3). Godliness is possessing a Christ-like character.

God has given us so many things that if we tried to keep track of it, they will be too numerous to count. One of the things that He has given us is the word of God.

Remember when God blew in the nostrils of Adam that was the breath of life entering into him. In one breath bodily organs were developed, blood flowed, the heart began to beat, the brain began to function and man became a living soul.

Isn't it also true that before someone passes away, they always release their last breath? The body of that person will decay, but the spirit and soul of that person will live forever. That soul will live eternally with God in Heaven or live eternally in Hell. The choice is clearly up to the individual.

The word of God is the breath of life for us. If we allow it to flow in our lives, our worship will be developed. Our prayer life will be developed. There will be an outward manifestation of Godliness seen within us.

I hope that you are a member of a church where the Spirit of God is allowed to move. If you are attending a church because of the number of seats it can hold but there is no seat for God to sit in, then you need to get into another church.

If you are in a church where the pastor is trained in allowing the Spirit of God to have *full control* of the service, then you are in a position to allow the Holy Spirit to have full control over you. The anointing that is allowed to flow in that ministry will flow through your life leading to healing, strength, and deliverance. These things are needed to bring you into Godliness.

Take a look at this Christ-like character in action:

Job had a Christ-like character, even in his suffering. Paul had a Christ-like character during persecution. Shadrach, Meshach, and Abednego had a Christ-like character when they were facing the fiery furnace. Daniel displayed a Christ-like character before, during, and after he was thrown in the lion's den. Paul and Silas had a Christ-like character while locked up in prison. The list goes on and on.

That claim should be said for all of us who are Disciples of Christ. Grant it, it's not going to be seen overnight but the more diligent we are at allowing a Christ-like character to be developed in us, the quicker it can be seen.

The only excuse we have is a willingness not to change. I don't know about you, but what good is it, if people can see my old nature displayed to the world.

There is no life in my old nature. But when I humble myself to walk in the light of God's word, Christ is seen. That's the true nature to be displayed to the world.

Do you remember the acronym W.W.J.D.? Which stands for **W**hat **W**ould **J**esus **D**o?

This would be good to remember as we proceed with our day. Learning to be conscious of what we say and display.

If you find yourself failing, stop what you are doing and repent. Get back on track and keep it moving.

God's grace and mercy will carry you, but be not deceived, the Bible does say, should I continue to sin that grace may abound, God forbid (Romans 6:1).

REFLECT ON THIS

Are you willing to allow Christ to be seen in your life?

Are you able to see where you have fallen short in this section?

What are people saying about your character?

CHAPTER SEVEN
BROTHERLY KINDNESS

Since we have accepted Jesus Christ as our Savior, this placed us into one big happy family. We have received the spirit of adoption (Romans 8:15). It's quite natural that when you grow up in a family with siblings, it's evident that someone is going to fight.

I guess the Lord said, well, I am going to let my children know that I will not tolerate this. Even though they are born from different parents and different cultures, I will not tolerate any fighting. After all, we will all be in Heaven together might as well get it right while we are down here on Earth.

Whether we like it or not, when we have accepted Jesus Christ as our personal Savior, this precious faith was breathed into all of us. We all have the same faith, which is a faith that believes Jesus Christ died for our sins and was raised again.

Could it have been possible that Peter was on to something when he said add brotherly kindness to your faith, after all, he was walking with Jesus along with the other Disciples learning how to be like Christ?

I can think of several brothers in the Bible that were not very good examples, such as Jacobs's boys. They put Joseph in a pit to die. Jacob and Esau had issues with each other because of their parents. Abimelech killed all his brothers, and of course, we can't forget about Cain who killed his brother Abel.

I'm thinking of Jonathan and David. Even though they were not blood brothers, they had brotherly kindness towards one another. This love is the love that I believe God wants from his children.

Jonathan could have turned against David to please his father, King Saul, but he didn't. David had brotherly kindness when he could have killed King Saul in the cave.

Sometimes a spirit can come over us for whatever reason and we grow a hatred for one another. That's a trick of the enemy. I don't know why people think the devil does not know the word of God. Who do you think misquoted the word of God when Jesus was in the wilderness?

The devil knows exactly what the Bible says, that's why he does everything in his power to keep us from reading it, especially the big lie that "man wrote the Bible." As long as the devil can blind people with this lie, the more he's not able to be exposed.

I know it's difficult to not allow people to get on our nerves. But someone is bound to aggravate you, after all, we are on this Earth with billions of other people.

This is a work in progress. People are moved to do and say some hurtful things but it's only because of who they are listening to. We have to develop an ear to hear God's voice and not the deceitful voice of the devil.

In other words, we have to have a caring attitude towards everyone as if they are our blood brothers and sisters.

Since these born-again believers were exiled from their homes, Peter encouraged them to be kind to one another. They were all going through the same suffering at the same time. They were all being tried in their faith.

They were all in this position because they were Christians. When the suffering gets worse, are you going to deny Christ and return to the world? This is why Peter had to send letters informing them that if you are suffering for righteousness sake, God will reward you (1 Peter 3: 13, 14). It is better to suffer for doing good than to suffer for being disobedient.

In some cases natural brothers and sisters fight and have a genuine dislike for each other but just know as a born-again believers, we cannot support this behavior or our prayers will not get answered (Psalm 66:18).

Someone has to be clothed in humility. Apologize, whether you feel like it's your fault or not, and get it right before God.

If we don't forgive, neither will our Father forgive our trespasses and sin (Matthew 6:15).

Brotherly kindness is diligently having a love for someone else, regardless of their flaws.

REFLECT ON THIS

Are you willing to suffer for righteousness?

Are you in a place right now to be your brother's keeper?

Are you compassionate?

CHAPTER EIGHT
LOVE

The last principle we will be discussing is love. For God so loved the world that He gave His only begotten Son that whosoever believeth in Him should not perish but have everlasting life (John 3:16).

Supplement your faith with love. 1 Corinthians Chapter 13 gives us a detailed description of what love is and the expectations of it.

The chapter speaks for itself but there is a specific breakdown starting from verses 4-8 and it gives a detailed description of the actions of love.

People throw that word around so much that they don't know what love means. Love goes beyond your feelings. If you are feeling great you say, "I love you." If everything is going well with your children you say, "I love you." If everything is great at home with your spouse you say, "I love you."

What happens when your children aren't acting the way they should, or your spouse is having a "bad day." Are you feeling like you love them? No. At the moment, your feelings are not agreeing with love. Your feelings are expressing anger, frustration, aggravation, etc.

Love suffers long. I know the Bible says you can be angry and sin not (Ephesians 4:26). But don't let it get to the point of hatred and revenge.

Perhaps you can walk away and take a breather. Put yourself on time-out.

Love will suffer for as long as it takes until you or someone else live according to the word of God.

God suffered with us when we rejected salvation, wanting to do our own thing. Other people suffered with us because of our bad attitudes or bad decisions.

Why is it that we want people to be longsuffering with us, but we don't want to be longsuffering with other people?

You know why? It's because we just don't feel like it. We want people to accept our mess and fix their mess so it won't come to us. God is not like that.

Love is patient. It endures all things. Believes all things. Hopes all things. Love will give people time to change and transform their lives according to the word of God.

This is where patience comes in. We have to allow love to do the work in others, while love is doing work within us. We have to be diligent in allowing this addition to our faith to be in full-blown operation.

This unconditional love should be given to others as God has given to us. Is it easy? No.

Can it be done? Yes.

The Bible says that I can do all things through Christ who strengthens me (Philippians 4:13).

We have to go through Christ for us to be able to love according to what is written in scripture. If we go through our feelings, the results will not be the same.

We run the risk of not winning someone to the Lord and displaying a wrong concept of Christianity.

The beginning of 1 Corinthians 14:1 says to follow after love. In other words, wherever love is headed, follow after it.

Love will never lead us into a place where we should not be. God is love (1 John 4:8) so as we follow love, we are following God.

REFLECT ON THIS

Are you a loving person? If not, why?

Do you see unconditional love at work in your life?

CONCLUSION

Peter along with James and John walked closely with Jesus (Matthew 17:1-8). They witnessed some things that the other disciples were not able to see.

Peter and the other disciples had normal lives just like anyone else. I'm sure during their day, the name of Jesus was heard among them.

They heard some great things about Jesus because when He showed up, they **left their homes** and followed Him.

Isn't it ironic that these disciples placed themselves in a position of leaving all to follow Christ as opposed to the believers that Peter was writing to who were **forced out** of their homes for following Christ?

In Peter's experience, before, during, and after Christ, he concluded that if we would just be diligent in reading scripture and add virtue, knowledge, temperance, patience, godliness, brotherly kindness, and love to our faith, we will not be barren or unfruitful in the knowledge of our Lord and Savior Jesus Christ.

We have to be diligent in learning about virtue, temperance, godliness, brotherly kindness, love, patience, biblical knowledge. There are going to be situations that come up in life and we are going to have to be knowledgeable in these areas for us to make it.

Peter made a statement before that, he said these things should be abounding in you.

Peter began to say that if these things are lacking in your life that you will be blind and unable to see afar off placing yourself in a position to forget that you were purged from sin.

If you have been saved long enough, you have at some point realized that when you don't connect with the word of God, you will begin to reconnect with your old self.

If you get too far into your old self, it will be hard for you to connect with God because your flesh won't be interested in a sacrificed life before God any longer.

If you find yourself in that position, you need to fight your way back to repentance and get right with God.

You cannot live separated from the word of God. You are born-again. You have to now live like the Bible is telling you to live.

Conclusion

Born-again believers should look and live as if we have been cut from the same cloth. If we believe in the same God. If we read the same Bible, then we all should be living the same way. Why do you say that?

> ***Because there is One Lord, one faith and one baptism, One God and Father of all, who is above all and through all and in you all. (Ephesians 4:5, 6, KJV).***

If your life does not look like it came from the Bible, something is wrong. I promise you, the failure is not on God's end.

Peter says that an entrance shall minister unto you abundantly into the everlasting Kingdom of our Lord and Savior Jesus Christ. I don't know if you caught that, but Peter is saying keep these things abounding in your life and you will be ushered in the Kingdom of God. Allow the word of God to change you.

I haven't sat down with Jesus and the Disciples by campfire traveling from town to town, but apparently, Peter summed it all up in just a few verses because he was there.

Peter knew that his time of departing Earth was coming soon that he said even after he's gone from the Earth, he will make sure that these things are preached. Please read 2 Peter 1:8-15.

People of God, it's time to shake off everything that is not about a life of Godliness. Heaven sounds like a glorious place to live and we ought to do all that we can to return there.

Come magnify the Lord with me, and let us exalt His name together, Psalm 34:3, KJV).

God Bless You

Special thanks to my loving husband, Willie, for your patience during this project. I thank God for you and your love for me because you have truly been an addition and blessing to my life.

To my children and grandson, I love you all very much and pray that you will allow God to reveal Himself to you as you travel through this life.

To my Dad, brothers, sisters, and extended family, I pray that this booklet will minister to your heart helping you to walk with the Lord. I wish mom could have been here to see this, but at least she's with the King, in Glory, Hallelujah!

To my Pastor, apostle Albert R. Oliver and Rev. Carolyn Oliver, thank you so much for allowing God to have His way in your life. The allowance of God in your life has taught the Elohim Christian Center family to allow God in their lives.

CPSIA information can be obtained
at www.ICGtesting.com
Printed in the USA
LVHW051931100521
687012LV00013B/671